D1630047

THE BRIGHTON LINE

John Eddolls

DAVID & CHARLES
Newton Abbot   London   North Pomfret (Vt)

Contents

Mainly for Sheila, Susan and John,
but with thoughts for those who
use the Brighton Line.

1   Early Days

On a sunny Easter Monday, in 1844, a crowded 45 carriage train worked by four locomotives noisily lurched from London Bridge. At both New Cross and Croydon a further six carriages plus a locomotive were added. Four-and-a-half hours later Brighton's first excursion train reached the resort.

One hundred years earlier the Sussex fishing village of Brighthelmstone was poor and unknown, until in 1750 Doctor Richard Russell from nearby Lewes wrote a book, in Latin, discussing the medicinal value of water from the sea. The book, which was titled *Dissertations concerning the use of sea water in the diseases of the glands*, not only recommended sea bathing in acceptable places such as Brighthelmstone, but went further by encouraging readers to drink the salt water in prescribed quantities. With a surprising swiftness bottles of Brighthelmstone water were on sale on the streets of London and soon the health conscious wealthy began to flock to the fresh and fashionable village.

A few years were to pass before George, the playboy Prince Regent, brought his Court to spend the summer in the growing town, seemingly to take the waters and to enjoy the agreeable Sussex climate, although doubtless he was anxious to rid himself of the ever watchful eye of his domineering father. Subsequently in 1787 the Prince instructed architect Henry Holland to build a Pavilion and as a result the future of Brighton as a resort was assured. The classical pavilion was constructed under the careful guidance of Holland, later to be garnished with pinnacles and a massive 130ft high onion-shaped dome to a flamboyant eastern design by John Nash.

The building cost Prince George over £500,000, a very considerable sum for those days. William Cobbett, the noted traveller and author of *Rural Rides* thought the Pavilion looked like 'half a turnip with four small ones at the corner'. Following his coronation in 1820 King George IV continued to visit Brighton until 1827 while his niece Queen Victoria wishing to familiarise herself with the various attractions offered stayed in the town during the early part of her reign – unlike her uncle, she found the lack of privacy tiring.

At the turn of the nineteenth century the 52-mile stage coach journey from London to Brighton took between four and five hours, and neither canal nor natural waterway linked the Capital with the resort. Furthermore, the planning of a suitable railway route was continually hampered by argument and frustration, as if a direct line were to be built it would be necessary to cross three formidable features, the North Downs, the Weald and the South Downs.

In the mid-1830s steam coaches were introduced to the heavily-used Brighton Road. These helped to speed the journey and had advantages in load-carrying and perhaps greater flexibility than horses, as if it became necessary to curtail the service through inclement weather steam coaches did not cost money to keep or feed. However, steam coaches did little to suppress the gathering demand for a fast rail link, a demand that was only satisfied when ambitious engineering schemes and speculative City backing led to the eventual

	Average Journey Time	3rd class Single Fare
LONDON BRIDGE ✳		
New Cross ✳		
Forest Hill		
Sydenham		
Penge		
Anerley		
Norwood		
Croydon ✳	20 mins	5½p
Stoat's Nest ✳		7p
Merstham Tunnel		
Merstham		9½p
Reigate Road ✳	48 mins	11p
Horley ✳		13p
Three Bridges ✳	65 mins	15½p
Balcombe Tunnel		
Balcombe		17p
Ouse Viaduct		
Haywards Heath ✳	90 mins	20p
Folly Tunnel		
Burgess Hill		22p
Hassocks Gate ✳		23p
Clayton Tunnel		
Patcham Tunnel		
BRIGHTON ✳	x 120 mins	27p

THE BRIGHTON LINE
1850

✳ Carriage and Horse
unloading facilities at
these stations

N

x Morning and afternoon direct
90 min. express
1st class – 65p, 2nd class – 52p

Brighton station – the main concourse around 1900 (Lens of Sutton)

construction of the Brighton line on a route planned by Sir John Rennie.

In 1835 an Act of Parliament authorised the incorporation of the London & Croydon Railway. The purpose of the railway was to construct a line for the $10\frac{1}{4}$ miles from Corbett's Lane, Bermondsey, on the London & Greenwich Railway, to West Croydon. The line was officially opened on 1 June 1839 and later proved the real basis of the London Brighton & South Coast Railway. The London & Greenwich line north of Corbett's Lane terminated at an uncovered two-platformed London Bridge (opened on 14 December 1836). While proving totally inadequate for the London & Croydon, it gave the company the opportunity of a toll levied passage to a City terminus. Later the Croydon obtained sanction to extend the cramped station.

The Brighton Act received Royal Assent on 15 July 1837, authorising the London & Brighton Railway to construct a 40-mile main line from Norwood on the London & Croydon Railway, to Brighton.

In devising his route, Rennie had 'smoothed over' the undulating contours of Southern England to produce a line of long flat stretches with gradual banks and gentle climbs. The day-to-day construction was supervised by Rennie's chief engineer, John Rastrick. Because of the progressive nature of the plan, considerable work and earth movement was necessary, including long tunnels at Merstham, 1831yd (North Downs), Balcombe, 1141yd (The Weald), and Clayton, 2259yd (South Downs), although the sweep of the 492yd Ouse Valley Viaduct (The Weald) crossing the soft Sussex countryside was the architectural achievement of the line. Despite these natural hazards the railway was completed in $3\frac{1}{2}$ years, a considerable feat of engineering by any standard.

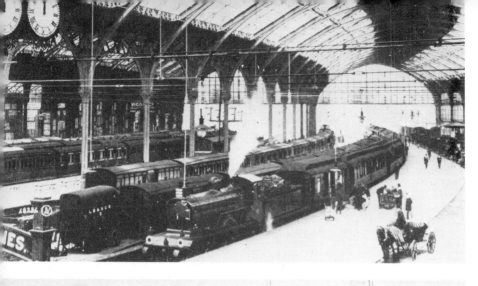

Top: *Brighton station in the early years of the century. A Class B4 4-4-0 stands at the eastern side of the station. The Pullman cars are those of the 1888 set. Note the fine station roof and the curving platforms* (Lens of Sutton)

Centre: *Busy Three Bridges about 1900 before the line was quadrupled. Note the East Grinstead branch train in the bay on the right and the engine shed on the left* (Lens of Sutton)

Bottom: *The six-platform Clapham Junction in the late 19th century. The mixed gauge track at what were then the West London line platforms on the right were for GWR broad gauge services* (Lens of Sutton)

Railway history to the south of London is complicated for three particular reasons. First, it was specifically laid down by Parliament that there should be only one railway outlet to the south of the City, and that any further development should be by way of a continuation of the Croydon line. Second, numerous territorial disputes between the various companies led to much confusion. Finally, many technical problems had to be overcome, as railway engineering was in its teething days.

Upon completion of the Norwood to Brighton stretch the London & Brighton sold the section of track between Coulsdon and Redhill to the South Eastern Railway. Therefore the somewhat bizarre situation arose that a Brighton train leaving London Bridge started out over the London & Greenwich (1836) to Corbett's Lane. From that point the train travelled to Norwood Junction over the London & Croydon (1839) and it was there that the London & Brighton (1841) commenced. But to complicate matters even further, the South Eastern Railway had running powers over the whole section from London Bridge to Coulsdon, and previously it had purchased that part of the Brighton line from Coulsdon to Redhill, the Brighton having negotiated running powers.

In 1846 the London & Brighton and London & Croydon Railways amalgamated to form the London Brighton & South Coast Railway, by which title the railway was known for the next 76 years.

The hugely successful Great Exhibition of 1851 was staged in London's Hyde Park. The centre of the Exhibition was a 21-acre glass palace designed by Joseph Paxton. When the Exhibition closed Paxton's 'Crystal Palace' was carefully dismantled and removed to Sydenham to an expansive site that had been purchased from a director of the LBSCR. It was anticipated that there would be a tremendous demand to visit the Palace on its new suburban site and as a result the West End & Crystal Palace Railway was formed, its London terminus being named Pimlico.

The Brighton company was the majority shareholder in the WE&CPR and certainly its shrewd investment proved worthwhile, for on special occasions upwards of 100,000 passengers a day would choke the trains routed to the Palace. It is interesting to note that the Crystal Palace stood at Sydenham until 1936 when the building was destroyed by fire, but well before then the district had taken its name. In the mid-nineteenth century the prestige-seeking Brighton company was anxious to establish a West End terminal and thoughts gravitated towards Waterloo. However, talks with the London & South Western Railway were both unhelpful and ineffective and the Brighton turned its attention on Pimlico, situated a mile further up the south bank of the River Thames.

Over the next decade many suburban routes were developed until a complete network began to evolve. These new lines included an extension by the LBSCR from Norwood Junction to Crystal Palace, thus gaining the

Top: *Selhurst Station towards the end of the nineteenth century and before the line was quadrupled, with a Brighton–Victoria train arriving* (Lens of Sutton)

Centre: *Class D3 0–4–4T No. 395 Gatwick on a suburban stopping train near Balham, about 1910. Originally, 36 locomotives of this type were built between 1892 and 1896* (Lens of Sutton)

Bottom: *Class B4 (R. J. Billinton) 4–4–0 No 49, a class of 33 locomotives built between 1899–1902, photographed near Coulsdon on a down South Coast Express. The mixed stock includes a Pullman car* (Lens of Sutton)

Brighton company a roundabout entry into Pimlico. The siting of this station on the south bank quickly proved unpopular with railway passengers and after operating for barely two years Pimlico closed and a new station was opened on the rapidly developing north side of the river. This station was named Victoria. During the same year, 1860, the Brighton received sanction for a direct spur from Windmill Bridge Junction, mid-way between East Croydon and Norwood Junction, to Wandsworth Common and in 1862 for a high-level line east of Clapham Junction, which, after winding above the LSWR main line into Waterloo, rejoined the original LBSCR path into Victoria. This final link afforded the completion of the route from London (Victoria) worked today.

Throughout Queen Victoria's long reign the bustling resort of Brighton continued to attract the ostentatious and the well-to-do. Towards the end of the nineteenth century wealthy City businessmen pioneered the now common practice of buying a seaside home and travelling daily to their London offices. The Brighton Railway had always been essentially a passenger-carrying line, as the town had neither natural harbour nor a particular industry to support. The company's

trains were filled by wealthy commuters, affluent holidaymakers, who would stay at the town's elegant sea-front hotels, and lastly, by the more plebian day-tripper on excursion tickets from the metropolis or its surrounds. The enormous gulf during these times in the country's class and social structure was unquestionably reflected in the LBSCR trains, and the Brighton wanted to be a luxury railway, with routes networking to the South Coast, and services calling at rural stations that furnished middle-class market towns.

In North America, George Pullman, a talented young businessman who had experienced appalling conditions on the American railroads, had taken it upon himself to design and build an experimental railway coach to an extremely high standard of comfort. The American railroads showed little interest in his project until after the assasination of President Lincoln, when Pullman was able to offer his coach quietly for the personal use of a distressed Mrs Lincoln, as she accompanied her dead husband's body across the United States for burial at his home town of Springfield.

Suddenly Pullman was famous, his organisation flourished and duly opened a subsidiary coach building works in Britain. The Midland Railway bought while the LBSCR at first watched with a cautionary interest, but in 1875 the first individual Pullmans ran on the Brighton line. In 1881 the Brighton purchased a set of Pullman stock to inaugurate its Pullman Limited Express. One car in the train, named *Beatrice*, was fitted with electric lights, the first on a railway carriage, powered by batteries which were recharged at Victoria from a steam generator between each trip. Despite the ambience the Limited managed to evoke, it was poorly supported from the start and was quickly subjected to ridicule and criticism. One major complaint was over the lack of privacy in the open parlour cars, which could so easily encourage young men to flirt with members of the opposite sex. An even stronger issue, particularly voiced by the pious, proclaimed that the train ran on Sundays, the day of rest when everybody, from traveller to engine driver, should have been worshipping in church. As a result the train gained the unfortunate nickname of the 'Sabbath Breaker'. But the Brighton was undaunted and although it curtailed the Sunday train, it persevered with its ideals by continuing to run single Pullman cars among rakes of ordinary coaches. In 1888 the company took delivery of a set of yet more luxurious Pullman stock in which sofas, scent and cigars were available to the travelling public and over the next ten years an overall relaxation in social attitudes allowed the introduction of an all-Pullman Sunday express called the Brighton Limited. This 1888 train was also notable for its enclosed flexible gangways between cars, the first corridors other than on Queen Victoria's LNWR royal saloons of 1869.

Around this period a much-needed improvement in running schedules was called for and subsequently introduced. In the early days there was really nothing that could be described as fast, and even the tighter schedules allowed between 70 and 80 minutes for the 51-mile run. Part of the problem centred around congestion in the Redhill area, where it will be recalled the South Eastern Railway had previously purchased the track from the LBSCR, and now used the facility extensively. The two railways operating on the same section of line led to complications and sometimes downright hostility. The trouble generally centred over passengers travelling with the alternative carrier's tickets.

In 1900 having suffered endless frustration concerning schedules and disagreements over revenue, the Brighton acted and opened a 6½-mile relief by-pass between Coulsdon and Earlswood, so avoiding the junction at Redhill. This loop, which necessitated the construction of a counterpart to Merstham Tunnel, was called the Quarry Line. It improved the timings by approximately ten minutes and handles through traffic today. Despite the advantage gained upon the completion of the Quarry line and the opportunity for even better schedules, the established 60-minute start-to-stop journey survived until after the end of the Southern Railway era, and it was the Southern's own outstanding General Manager, Sir Herbert Walker who strongly advocated Brighton trains 'Every hour, On the hour, In the hour.'

On 1 November 1908, a new seven-coach all-Pullman train was introduced – the Southern Belle. This train created an unusual precedent in railway circles as it was the Pullman coaching stock that was named Southern Belle and not the particular train service. This example of dedicating coaches exclusively to a specific train was later adopted by its electric successor, the aptly titled Brighton Belle.

Much to the irritation of first-class passengers, third-class Pullmans were launched in September 1915 and gradually as the years passed the number of first-class seats declined, giving way to a less elaborate, yet still luxurious third. This reduction in first-class compartments not only applied to the Pullmans but also to the conventional LBSCR stock trains, and although the frequency now offered by the timetable was acceptable to most, many grumbled over the deplorable lack of corridor coaches on ordinary trains and pointed out that the Brighton stock rode with a noticeable bounce. It was popularly supposed that this uncomfortable ride and the somewhat spartan conditions that the third-class

Above: *Class B4X 4–4–0 No 71, rebuilt from Class B4 in 1923, thunders up Forest Hill bank with the down City Limited. The ten-coach express includes a Pullman Car. Photographed about 1925* (Lens of Sutton)

Below: *Class B4X 4–4–0 No 60 races through Norwood Junction en route for London Bridge, with the up City Limited* (Lens of Sutton)

passenger suffered, was in order to keep costs down by building the stock as light as possible. Following the end of World War I, commuting on the Brighton began in earnest, and businessmen were especially catered for by the up and down City Limited, both of which had a high proportion of first class seats, and some coaches had corridors. Even in 1933, when the line was electrified by the Southern Railway, the new electric trains forming the equivalent City Limited service were made up into rakes of two six-car units, each having seats for 120 third- and 138 first-class passengers, an unthinkable seating structure for today's functional rush-hour trains.

It is worthy of note in these competitive times, that British-designed and built locomotives always have been, and hopefully, always will be, in unfailing demand. Certainly the High-Speed Inter-City 125 design and other

Above: *Marsh 4–4–2 of Class H1, built 1905–1906, No 38 passes through South Croydon with a South Coast express. This type of locomotive worked Oxted line trains until 1951* (Pamlin Prints)

Below: *Class 13 Marsh 4–4–2 express tank No 79, one of a class of 27, working the Southern Belle on the Quarry line* (Lens of Sutton)

technology are sought after and exported to many countries. In the LBSCR days many remarkable locomotives were built at Brighton Works under a passing array of locomotive superintendents. To select an engineer at random and suggest his work excelled is difficult, as all brought fame to the Works; nevertheless, perhaps three names particularly conjour memories of 'Brighton Steam', and for having produced some of the prettiest and best.

William Stroudley whose work influenced many of his contemporaries, took on the job in 1870. Following his appointment he was astonished to find 233 locomotives of 72 different classes in use, with little inter-changeability of parts. He quickly set to work on a

Class E5 0–6–2T No 591, built April 1904 and originally named Tillington. *Withdrawn November 1954.* Tillington *was the last 'Yellow' locomotive to serve on the LBSCR, and was one of a class of 30 used on fast passenger services. It is*

seen here between East Croydon and South Croydon. The train is composed of Balloon stock, so named for the highly-arched coach roofs (Lens of Sutton)

rationalisation programme and reduced the number of types to seven. Possibly his most successful designs were for the A1 Terrier Class 0–6–0 tank engine, built primarily for London suburban passenger duties, and for the powerful 0–4–2 Gladstones which were used exclusively for express traffic. The original *Gladstone* is preserved at York Railway Museum, while Terriers serve today on the Bluebell Railway, the Kent & East Sussex Railway and in the Isle of Wight.

Douglas Earle Marsh was appointed in 1904 and his large and imposing H Class Atlantics were frequently seen heading Oxted line trains until near the final days of steam. Marsh, also designed the celebrated Class I3 4–4–2 express tank locomotives. These were widely acclaimed, and soon found their way on to all sorts of fast services.

Lawson Billinton succeeded Marsh in 1911 and amongst his impressive locomotive designs was the splendidly handsome 4–6–4 express tank. No 333 of this class was named *Remembrance* after those company employees killed in the 1914–18 war.

All the LBSCR superintendents were individual in their approach, method

and design. Stroudley, though a particularly exacting man was always prepared to listen to his subordinates; he would ride in the cab and was well respected by his crews. He delighted in bestowing names on his locomotives, but then Marsh took charge and chose to give his none. Stroudley painted his passenger locomotives a deep yellow, but Marsh favoured a dull chocolate brown.

In the London Brighton & South Coast Railway's final years of independence the company continued to expand and by 1923 had no fewer than 495 locomotives. Railway advertisements influenced the public and suggested they travel to Paris via Newhaven/Dieppe, or spend a day by the 'Sunny South Coast', while others told prospective home-buyers of the good life in the healthy Surrey Hills.

Throughout its history the Brighton was progressive, yet prudent, encrusted with tradition, yet bursting with individuality. At the end, a member of the Board was of the opinion that it was, 'the most marvellously efficient organisation known to this century's industry'. Be he right or wrong, the balance sheet certainly highlighted how well the company had done.

2 The Southern Railway and the Brighton Pullmans

The Southern Railway came into being on 1 January 1923 and over the next decade did more to suburbanise Southern England than any other institution ever had, or probably ever will. The company worked hand-in-glove with the major property developers by encouraging families to set-up homes in the South. The campaign flourished, but undoubtedly the greatest boost came in the Chairman's announcement to shareholders on 27 February 1930 detailing main line electrification for the 36 miles of railway from Coulsdon through to the South Coast.

Previously the progressive LBSCR had electrified the track between London and Coulsdon by an overhead wire system supplying alternating current at 6,700 volts, but in 1929, the Southern converted this to the third-rail method, working off a direct current at 660 volts. It was this system the Southern now planned to adopt.

It was a sad farewell to the Atlantics, the 4–6–4 express tanks and the tiny but powerful Terriers, for steam had served railway and passenger well, especially in the closing years when handsome King Arthur 4–6–0s were booked to haul the latest steel-panelled bogie stock, the complete express meticulously finished in spotless livery of dark green. In dormitory land, with its creosoted toolsheds and neatly mown back lawns, electrics silenced the home-coming hiss of nearing steam and the busy sound of clanking coupling rods. It also ended slip-coach workings to the more remote rural stations from non-stop coast trains. Nevertheless, despite the onslaught of modernisation it was possible to reach Brighton by steam train, via the roundabout Oxted, Uckfield and Lewes branch until the mid-1960s, when the famed Battle of Britain and West Country class locomotives brought a dash of excitement to this modest branch. In

Above: *Class L comprised seven express 4–6–4 tanks, built between 1914 and 1922. No 333* Remembrance *in Southern Railway colours, speeds the Southern Belle through the Downs at Patcham* (Lens of Sutton)

Left: *Introduced in 1926, Maunsell King Arthur class 4–6–0 No 795* Sir Dinadan *heads the 10-coach Southern Belle on the Quarry Line towards the sea. These distinguished locomotives were used until electrification on the Brighton expresses* (Lens of Sutton)

Centre: *Marsh Atlantic, Class H2 No B421 on the Southern Belle at Merstham in the North Downs – about 1925* (Lens of Sutton)

Bottom: *The Brighton Belle (Unit 3053), at speed near South Croydon, 20 May 1956* (Pamlin Prints)

1969 the Uckfield–Lewes line was closed.

To feed the Brighton/Worthing electrification scheme the Southern built 20 six-coach corridor sets (6PUL), each set containing a Pullman car with both first- and third-class accommodation. Four 225hp motors powered each motor coach. For semi-fast and slow workings the Company provided 33 four-car sets formed of three third-class non-corridor coaches and one composite coach with corridor and toilet facilities and classified 4LAV. The motor coaches were powered by two 275hp motors. Additionally, special units were produced to meet the requirements of the Brighton Belle and the City Limited and it was during these formative years of electric traction that the unique Southern Railway terminology for categorising types of electric stock was first used. The Southern Region has upheld this custom of classing electric multiple-units by a single digit indicating the number of vehicles making up the unit, followed by three letters of descriptive identification, although today's electric stock carries an official British Rail classification as well.

Following the successful completion of the Brighton contract the Southern board was well-pleased when on a sunny Whitsun weekend in June 1933, 130,000 passengers packed the Brighton line trains.

For its next electrification scheme the Southern decided to extend the third rail to Hastings, via Lewes and Eastbourne, and for this project the Company built 17 six-car sets (6PAN) which included a first-class coach with a pantry/kitchen compartment. From the pantry staff employed by the Pullman Company served light refreshments throughout the set. Upon the launch of the 6PAN sets the Southern decided to mix the two types of electric express stock and over the next three decades, main line trains

on fast South Coast workings were generally formed of 12 coaches – one 6PUL Unit, the other a 6PAN.

One beneficial inovation following the introduction of electric trains was the arrangement of easily recognisable headcodes. A particularly useful facet relating to Central Division services was that even numbers terminated at Victoria, odd at London Bridge. This was especially helpful to travellers joining London trains that did not carry roof boards, and by and large electric trains did not.

The only other class of express electric stock occasionally seen working the Brighton line were the four-coach corridor units (4COR) together with sister sets 4BUF (with buffet). This stock differed from the earlier types in that when the units were coupled together it was possible for passengers to cross between sets and so walk the length of a twelve coach train, whereas no corridor connection joined the sets of class 6PUL or 6PAN.

4CORs were first built in 1937 to work the newly electrified Portsmouth line and became nicknamed 'Nelsons', not because of their primary destination, but due to the single window fronting the driver's compartment. This was sited next to the locked corridor connection, which swayed restlessly with the motion of the train. These units were to become the most highly regarded electric stock on the Southern Railway and the general appearance of today's express is not dissimilar. One 4COR set is preserved by the Southern Electric Group on the Nene Valley Railway, if only to be hauled by steam.

The last steam-hauled Southern Belle, left Victoria for Brighton at 15.05 on the afternoon of 31 December 1932. Appropriately the locomotive in charge was 4–6–4T No 2333 *Remembrance*.

For its all-electric Brighton Railway the Southern had previously taken delivery of three, five-car Pullman sets

Class L 4–6–4T No 327 in charge of the City Limited thunders up Forest Hill bank. This locomotive, together with the rest of its class, was rebuilt in 1935 to a Class N15X 4–6–0 tender locomotive and survived until 1956 (Lens of Sutton)

6PAN unit 3023 at London Bridge on a Brighton semi-fast evening commuter service, 12 August 1964. 6PAN and 6PUL units were operational until the mid-1960s, when they were replaced by 4CIG and 4BIG units (Pamlin Prints)

A Brighton up stopping train near Haywards Heath, hauled by Gladstone 0–4–2 No 172, during the mid-1920s (Lens of Sutton)

(5BEL) two of which were used to form the express, while the remaining unit acted as standby. Each motor coach was powered by four 225hp motors whereby a total output of 900hp was produced to propel a five-car set. Externally the coaches were painted in Pullman chocolate-and-cream. The somewhat outdated practice of both naming and numbering first-class vehicles, yet allocating numbers only to the third-class coaches was retained. The first class cars were *Audrey, Doris, Gwen, Hazel, Mona, and Vera.* The powerful new electric Pullman express was booked to complete the journey in a leisurely 60 minutes and was scheduled for departure from Victoria at 11.00, 15.00 and 19.00, returning from Brighton at 13.25, 17.25, and 20.25.

Internally the train was lavishly equipped with plush armchair seating, detailed inlaid woodwork enhanced the doors and walls, and welcoming table-lamps were carefully placed at each compartment window. A comprehensive menu was available on all timings, plus an additional luncheon selection on mid-day trains, and all items, no matter how small, were served to tables covered with spotless white linen.

In June 1934 a policy decision resulted in the trains change of name to the Brighton Belle, a directive it is reported that was well received by the Brighton Corporation. Following an enforced six year rest during World War II, much needed and improved bogies were fitted in 1955, but in 1969 the regretable step of repainting the coaches in BR Inter-City livery was taken. Three years later the cost of further modernisation and extensive refurbishment was considered too enormous for BR to meet and in May 1972, the Brighton Belle, despite local protest, was withdrawn. For the Sussex resort and the people of Brighton it meant that approaching a century of service by Pullman and titled trains, with the ambience they had managed to create, the regular clientele they had gathered, the fierce arguments with the Pullman Company over the exclusion of kippers from the breakfast menu, all came to an abrupt end.

While no all-Pullman service regularly worked to London Bridge an electric City Limited took-over from

steam on 1 January 1933, and was formed with a high proportion of first-class accommodation, plus Pullman facilities. The service left Brighton at 8.45am and returned from London Bridge at 5.00pm. Three sets of six coaches (6CIT) were dedicated for use on this train, and as with the Belle, one unit acted as spare. For several years following the cessation of World War II a fast Brighton train left London Bridge at 5.00pm, but it quickly became a mere shadow of the former express.

Changes in commuting patterns led to additional stops being introduced and in a strangely unpublicised fashion, and with surprisingly little fuss, the 5.00pm Brighton slipped out of service and never returned.

Gatwick Airport station in the early 1960s. A two-coach (2HAL) Victoria service prepares to depart. These units had an all-steel exterior construction and were pleasing to the eye, but the interiors were relatively sparsely furnished (Lens of Sutton)

10.18 Victoria–Portsmouth Harbour (4COR+4BUF+4COR), at Christ's Hospital on the Mid-Sussex line – 2 September 1951. All trains on this service are now routed via East Croydon and Gatwick and run under Headcode 8 (Pamlin Prints)

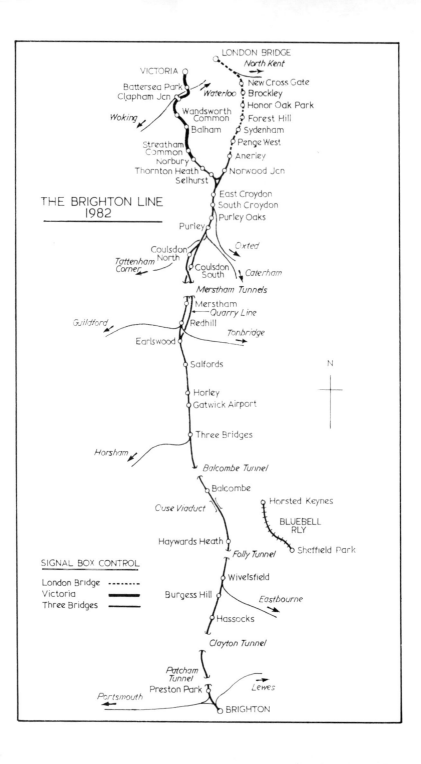

3   Into the Eighties

All electric stock on the Central Division was built before 1973 and some elderly suburban units originally served in Southern green. Cautious budgeting and conservative housekeeping dating back to the earliest LBSCR days has resulted in many usable parts from buffers to bogies and couplings to luggage racks being carefully removed before the rolling stock is broken-up for scrap. Subsequently the salvaged parts are completely reconditioned and fitted to a vehicle under construction. A number of simple wooden picture frames, decorating compartment walls today, were fashioned by craftsmen nearly 80 years ago. These frames have quickly become scarce and are now a modest but sort-after collector's piece, with the inevitable reproductions confusing the market.

Southern electric stock works in sets of two or four pre-coupled coaches, thereby forming an electric multiple-unit of corresponding length. Six types service the main Brighton line and five others feed its branches. All Brighton line express stock is painted British Rail Inter-City blue-and-grey and is allocated to Brighton (BI). South Coast trains are normally formed of three, four-coach units and one unit generally includes a buffet car. Each four-coach unit is powered by four 250hp motors and all classes of main line rolling stock can work with the alternative types of long-distance stock.

The oldest express type operating is Class 411 (Southern Region 4CEP). Launched in 1955 and built primarily for the Kent Coast electrification scheme, the coaches were assembled at Eastleigh on Ashford underframes. The sister unit, Class 410 (4BEP) includes a buffet car. The riding qualities of both classes was never particularly good, and

has with age become increasingly poor. However, cash limits have dictated that no new stock is available for South Coast trains, and faced with this problem BREL engineers are undertaking a massive refurbishment programme, the first of which relates to Classes 410 and 411 Kent Coast stock.

The current refurbishing programme is expected to reach the Brighton line by the mid-1980s and it is estimated that the work will double the life of the rolling stock. Whilst the reconditioned units will never equal the standard of Inter-City trains, the vehicles will be completely overhauled, insulated with fibreglass and fitted with the latest anti-glare double glazing. The coaches will have electronic temperature controls, a much-needed public address system, improved toilets, Inter-City type seats and flourescent lighting. For the driver, measures have been taken to increase comfort and an electrically-heated high-impact glass windscreen is being installed.

The supposedly more modern but visually similar Class 421 (4CIG) was built at York, primarily for the Southern's Central Division. Matching Class 420 (4BIG) is provided with a buffet car. Interestingly the IG part of the classification derives from the old LBSC telegraphic code for Brighton. Introduced in 1964, Classes 420 and 421 have improved bogies, which reward the passenger with a softer ride, and differ externally from the earlier 410 and 411 units by having a slightly rounded glass-fibre front to the driving cabs.

With identical fronts to the Class 421 units the latest type of main line stock is the semi-fast Class 423 (4VEP) which was introduced in 1967. Built at York, primarily for long-distance commuter

Class 33 No 33048 heads a down London Bridge–Uckfield evening train past a 4EPB on an up Tattenham–London Bridge service, at South Croydon on 6 May 1981

work, the coaches are fitted with high density 2+3 seating and have doors at each bay. Good acceleration and smooth suspension has ensured that the units are well suited to their task, but in crowded conditions the seating can be noticeably cramped. Partly due to a shortage of rolling stock there seems no clear pattern in train formation and sets of Class 423 coupled with express Class 421 is commonplace, when perhaps a whole train formed of Class 421 would be far more acceptable; if only for appearance sake!

Gatwick Airport has its own version of the 4VEP designated Class 427 (4VEG), converted from 4VEP, which have a number of seats replaced by luggage racks. Externally the units have the rail/air link insignia plainly painted in large white letters beneath the driver's cab, but like the other electric units these multiples turn up everywhere, mixed with different classes of stock.

Most Brighton line suburban stock is allocated to Selhurst Depot (SU). Until recently suburban trains have differed from main line trains on two counts. Certain types of electric multiple unit

comprise two coaches, and while until 1980 all suburban units were painted plain blue, a change of heart in the spring of that year resulted in a decision to outshop local stock in Inter-City colours, with the exception of the Class 405 units. While this judgement is questionable, as it cancels the fundamental difference emphasising alternative types of trains, it certainly improves the outward image of the suburban stock.

There remains the one class that is to stay BR blue. Class 405 (4SUB) units were constructed at Eastleigh on frames from Lancing, and prototype units entered service as long ago as 1946. 4SUBs have a simple method of air-braking that differs from the newer electro-pneumatic system and accordingly cannot work with other classes of stock. They are fitted with four 250hp motors and do not give the smoothest ride at speed. These sets, which will be among the first to be replaced by more modern coaches, remain painted all-blue. However in 1982 to mark the passing of an era 4SUB unit No. 4732 was repainted green and lettered 'Southern' in the gold 'sunshine' lettering of the Southern Railway. All the 4SUB units were expected to be withdrawn by the end of 1983.

Suburban Classes 415 (4EPB) and 416 (2EPB) were built at Eastleigh during the 1950s and are of similar appearance to the older Class 405, but can be distinguished by the rain guttering skirting the coach roof. As with the other classes of electric multiple unit a 250hp motor is provided for each vehicle carried in the set and this type of multiple-unit can work with electric express stock. When Class 415 and 416 units become due for periodic repaint and overhaul, a number of sets are undergoing complete interior redecoration, including the installation of flourescent lights. A public address system is also provided, which when first used caused impassive City commuters to stir with surprise!

The last two variations of local stock are Class 418(2SAP) based at Selhurst and Class 414(2HAP) which are apportioned to Brighton. The two classes were originally built during the mid-1950s for semi-fast medium-distance work, and both types include a non-connecting corridor coach with a fitted toilet compartment, although on the Class 418 units the toilet more often remains locked. First-class compartments on Class 418 have been downgraded to second, as this stock now works principally on London Suburban lines. The 2HAPs have retained their first-class accommodation as they serve the medium-haul coastways route and occasionally the main London line. The letter classification is somewhat obscure but derives from the 1930s 2HAL (Half lavatory equipped) units. The letter P denotes electro-pneumatic brakes, and the letter S second class only by a process of substitution.

Just as it appears that the Southern Region is the Cinderella of British Rail, with its tired electric stock, the same indictment can readily apply to its fleet of little over 200 diesel locomotives. The mostly mundane and rather elderly locomotives found on the Brighton line are likely to be seen anywhere south of the Thames. Of course to be fair the 'Southern' is primarily an electric railway.

British Rail locomotives carry five-digit numbers. The first two digits relate to the locomotive class, the remaining three indicating the individual number. All passenger locomotives are painted blue with yellow ends and those operating from certain prestige-seeking sheds have eye-catching painted silver roofs as well.

In the formative days of diesel locomotive engineering numerous transmission failures occurred when the thrust of the direct drive diesel system proved too powerful for the locomotive wheels. As a result of fresh thinking the diesel-electric locomotive was introduced. By this method the mechanical power of a diesel engine is converted into electricity by a generator and fed to traction motors.

This form of propulsion has demonstrated both greater reliability and considerably increased flexibility. There are three classes working daily on the Brighton line, two of which use the diesel-electric system. First, and most often seen, are the workhorses of the Southern Region, the Class 33. Built by the Birmingham Railway Carriage & Wagon Company, and powered by Sulzer 1550hp diesel engines the locomotives weigh 76 tons and have a maximum speed of 85mph. Introduced in 1960 and nicknamed 'Cromptons' as the traction motors came from the Crompton Parkinson Works, they have converted many sceptics and shown their worth as reliable and efficient, but perhaps uninspiring locomotives. Class 33 locomotives can be used on passenger and freight duties but the type's greatest restriction when working passenger

Above: *4BEP 7005 bustles through South Croydon on a Littlehampton–Victoria express service, Easter Monday 1981*

Right: *4CIG 7373 leads an eight-coach 4CIG/4BIG formation on an up Eastbourne–Victoria express working off the Quarry line and past suburban electric multiple units in the sidings at Coulsdon North*

Bottom right: *Signal check – 33027 Earl Mountbatten of Burma is halted at South Croydon with the 17.04 from East Grinstead*

rosterings is its pulling power, limited to a rake of ten coaches. Class 33 locomotives are only loaned to the Central Division, as officially they are based at Eastleigh (EH) in the South Western Division, and at Hither Green (HG) in the South Eastern Division.

To meet specific territorial needs certain Class 33 locomotives have been adapted and sub-divided into three categories, Class 33/0, Class 33/1 and Class 33/2. The 33/0 is the basic type, Class 33/1 is modified for push/pull operation with emu trailer sets for services between Bournemouth and Weymouth Town and Waterloo and Salisbury, while Class 33/2 have narrow bodies for duties through the very tight tunnels between Tonbridge and Hastings.

Class 33s are booked to handle three up and three down peak-hour trains on the East Grinstead branch and can be seen taking this service, and going splendidly, between London Bridge and South Croydon. One great advantage of the class is that it is easily interchangeable with electric stock as the braking systems are compatible, and

during extreme weather conditions, Class 33s have frequently rescued stranded electric trains. Ninety-eight locomotives of this class have been built. Recent BR policy has resulted in a decision to name a selection of Class 33 locomotives and by the spring of 1983 five bore names: 33 008 *Eastleigh*, 33 025 *Sultan*, 33 027 *Earl Mountbatten of Burma*, 33 052 *Ashford*, 33 056 *The Burma Star*.

The younger and more powerful Class 47 locomotives are blessed with tigerish good looks, and although this type has been in widespread use for a number of years, until the late 1970s they seldom ventured to the Brighton tracks and regrettably, even by 1983, none was allocated to the Southern Region. Equally at home on long-distance express passenger trains or in charge of snaking loads of heavy oil wagons, many of these locomotives have been named, and Class 47s from depots scattered across the country power the twice-daily Brighton/Manchester passenger trains. By doing so they have brought a hint of romance to the Brighton line, for it is nice to see a

Brighton train hauled by *Robin Hood*! First built in 1962 by the Brush Traction Company, these locomotives have 2580hp Sulzer diesel engines and weigh 117 tons. The locomotives can easily attain speeds of up to 95mph. Although these locomotives were originally fitted with identification roller blinds, they did not carry headcodes applicable to the Central Division. These blinds have since been removed and the headcode boxes fitted with glass panels showing two white lights.

The last category of locomotive regularly seen on the line, other than those used solely for shunting purposes, is the Class 73 electro-diesel. These Jacks-of-all-trades, very much all-Southern Region products, were introduced in 1962. They weigh 75 tons and have a maximum speed of 90mph. They are powered by four 400hp English Electric traction motors for third-rail operation, plus a 600hp English Electric diesel engine for use on non-electrified lines. Forty-eight were built – their main depot is Stewarts Lane (SL) in Battersea.

Although Class 73s are used primarily on freight duties, for the operative period of the 1979 summer timetable, an accute shortage of electric stock led to locomotives of this class working the up 07.04 and 08.06 Brighton–London Bridge services and the 16.55 and 17.55 London Bridge–Brighton returns, when despite a sometimes jerky ride these electro-diesels undoubtedly proved that they could move. This surely must be the first occasion since electrification in 1932 that locomotive-hauled coaching stock has been in daily use on London to Brighton trains.

In keeping with the current vogue, three locomotives of this class have been named. 73 142 is called *Broadlands*. It is customary to roster this locomotive for special duties within the confines of the Southern Region, which include working the Royal trains and meeting visiting heads of state at Gatwick. In 1980, an unusually sad assignment was to take Earl Mountbatten's funeral train from Waterloo to his beloved Hampshire home at Romsey. A year later it was a happier occasion when it hauled the Royal Wedding train from Waterloo to Romsey for Prince Charles

No. 47077 North Star, *works the Brighton–Manchester service on the slow line through the Gloucester Triangle, at Croydon on 30 April, 1981*

and his bride. No 73 101 was named *Brighton Evening Argus* on 3 December 1980 to mark the centenary of the Brighton newspaper. This locomotive is often on standby at notable events. These chosen locomotives take turns with routine jobs and consequently *Broadlands* was allocated to London Bridge for empty stock work on some mornings during 1982. On 1 December 1982 No 73 129 was dubbed *City of Winchester*.

BR has announced that in 1984, Class 73s will operate a new dedicated Victoria–Gatwick Service. The locomotives will work from the 'country' end with push-pull rakes of revamped ex Western Region Mark II coaches finished in an experimental livery. Converted Class 414 (2HAP) driving trailers will front the London end.

Nearly all shunting duties on the line are in the capable care of the box-like, striped yellow and black faced, class 08 and 09 locomotives. These robust locomotives, developed from a standard LMS design of 1945, busily labour around the few remaining goods yards in Southern England. The class 08 was introduced in 1956 and is powered by an English Electric 350hp engine. The locomotives, built in British Rail Workshops, weighs 49 tons and have a maximum speed of 20mph. The 09, also built by British Rail, is alike in most details but has a higher maximum speed of 27mph. Both types are allocated to Selhurst (SU).

The end of an era for the non-electrified Oxted line came on 18 June 1962, for it signalled the gradual withdrawal of steam. On that day the first of 19 specially built three-car diesel-electric multiple-units entered service. These new sets, Class 207, were to share the workload with the 33s. Basically, the Class 207s were similar in external appearance to the class 205 units, although the cab fronts had more rounded corners. The 205s, which were busily working in Hampshire and had been since 1957, differed internally as they were furnished with 2+2 seating as opposed to the 3+2 seats found in the earlier stock. The more comfortable interior arrangement on the 207s was though not provided for the benefit of passengers, but was necessary as the coach width was narrower at 8ft 6in rather than the normal 9ft to permit operation through the restricted tunnels between Tonbridge and Tunbridge Wells West. The sets also differed in formation as the toilet composite coach was the middle vehicle, whereas it was a driving trailer on the 205s. Some of these Hampshire sets came onto Oxted branch workings after line closures in the Southampton area.

The riding qualities of both classes is not good, and the newer stock is particularly poor, the passenger in the motor coach especially experiencing a lively journey! Noise and vibration are also a tiring feature, and doubtless commuters given a choice would opt for the comparative luxury of a locomotive-hauled train.

Classes 205 and 207 are based at St Leonards. The units, powered by 600hp motors, were built at Eastleigh on underframes constructed at Ashford. The inverted black triangle on the front of the motor cab indicates that luggage space is available in that vehicle.

Locomotive-hauled trains on the Oxted branch consist of one first-class vehicle of BR Mark 2 type plus seven second-class coaches of Mark 1 design. Some seating springs in these Mark 1 coaches are worn and can sag but the stock was built in an age when quality

Above: *Down 17.36 Victoria–Uckfield train near East Croydon, on 5 June 1981. The first two sets are older Class 205 (Hampshire) units, while the rear is a Class 207 (Oxted) unit*

Right: *A 4VEP passes Norwood Yard on a Brighton–London Bridge stopping service. To the west 4SUBs wait at Selhurst Depot; to the south rise the tall office blocks of Croydon. 19 April 1981*

was paramount, and despite daily commuter use the coaches manage to retain a certain charm, the compartment walls being tastefully veneered in lightly polished wood; beware, though, the electric lighting, which is to say the least poor at night. Mark 1 coaches are also used on the Brighton–Manchester train, although in 1982 sleek Mark 2 London Midland Region Inter-City vehicles were introduced on certain trains. Additionally, some trains on this long distance working convey a buffet car, which must come as a relief to many a weary traveller, for much as this North–South train is welcome, it remains a stranger to good time-keeping.

On Monday 8 May 1978 the Central Division introduced a drastically modified timetable. Until then, apart from minor adjustments to schedules, the service had remained unaltered since World War II and Southern Railway days. Significant changes in travelling patterns, at both peak and off-peak periods necessitated this fresh approach to long established routes and customs.

The whole operation, including a seemingly pointless decision to revise headcodes, was skilfully advertised by placards, leaflets and constant station announcements, so that well before 'all change' day most toughened travellers knew what to expect, whilst the authorities leaned hard on customer loyalty, and pointed out, 'No rehearsal is possible, regular passengers MUST be fully prepared' Ultimately the day proved to be an anti-climax. There were a few justified grumbles and it was grudgingly admitted that a few services did run late, but by and large the new workings brought improved timings, especially for stopping trains.

However, as is mirrored in many walks of life, the railways over recent years have suffered a marked decline in the quality of service; first-class facilities have been reduced, the Pullmans have gracefully retired. In the early 1960s a white-jacketed steward toured the length of Brighton line fast trains serving pure ground coffee and fresh dairy cream into pleasant green china cups; today passengers collect refreshments from a laminated buffet car where dried coffee mixed with powdered milk is dispensed in a plastic mug – always assuming a buffet car is provided on the train.

PRINCIPAL BRIGHTON MAIN LINE TRAINS

To and from Victoria

Route	Headcode	Style	Facilities
Quarry	4	Fast	Buffet car
Quarry	14	Semi-fast	Buffet car on most trains
Quarry	24	Stopping	—
Redhill	34	Semi-fast	—
Redhill	44	Stopping	—

To and from London Bridge

Route	Headcode	Style	Facilities
Quarry	5	Fast	—
Quarry	15	Semi-fast	—
Quarry	25	Stopping	—
Redhill	35	Semi-fast	—
Redhill	45	Stopping	—
Crystal Palace and Redhill	95	Stopping	—

PRINCIPAL BRIGHTON LINE BRANCH LINE TRAINS

Destination	Route	Headcode	Style	Facilities
VICTORIA TO:				
Littlehampton	Quarry Hove	2	Fast	Buffet
Bognor	Quarry Horsham	6	Semi-fast	—

Class 73 electro-diesel No 73 125 works a track maintenance train between Purley and Purley Oaks on 6 June 1981

Portsmouth	Quarry Horsham	8	Semi-fast	Some services include Buffet
Reigate	Redhill	10	Stopping	—
Gatwick	Quarry	20	Fast	—
Littlehampton	Quarry Horsham	22	Semi-fast	—
Gatwick	Redhill	30	Semi-fast	—
Littlehampton	Redhill Horsham	32	Stopping	—
Bognor Regis	Redhill Littlehampton	36	Semi-fast	—
Eastbourne	Quarry Plumpton	50	Fast	Buffet
Newhaven Harbour	Quarry Plumpton	52	Fast	Some services include Buffet
East Grinstead	Oxted	66	Stopping from East Croydon	DEMU
Uckfield	Oxted	88	Stopping from East Croydon	DEMU

LONDON BRIDGE TO:				
Littlehampton	Quarry Hove	3	Fast	One evening train includes Buffet
Reigate	Redhill	11	Stopping	—
Portsmouth	Redhill	19	Stopping	—
Eastbourne	Quarry Plumpton	51	Fast	One evening train includes Buffet
East Grinstead	Oxted	77	Stopping from East Croydon	Class 33 hauled
Caterham/ Tattenham Corner	Forest Hill	93		2nd class only
Caterham/ Tattenham Corner	Forest Hill	97		2nd class only
Uckfield	Oxted	99	Stopping from East Croydon	Class 33 or DEMU

4 Calling at All Stations

London Bridge Station is a lonely place even on a cheerful summer's day, and to make matters worse during the winter months the City worker is often accompanied by a biting wind as he strides across the bridge.

Badly damaged by German bombs in December 1940 the sixteen-platform station was rebuilt and officially reopened on 14 December 1978. London's first railway station (London & Greenwich Railway, 1836) was sited where the ticket office stands today. Subsequently enlarged, part of the LBSCR workmanship can still be seen in the interesting figured brickwork on the wall alongside platform 9.

The Southern Region South Eastern Division controls platforms 1 to 6, with trains passing through from Cannon Street, Waterloo East and Charing Cross, whereas platforms 7 to 16 of the main terminus cater for the Central Division. The Central Division handles over 500 trains a day at London Bridge, bringing 75,000 passengers crowding through the barriers, mostly travelling to or coming home from work.

There is widespread belief that as the train eases away from the platform at London Bridge that it heads south for Sussex and the sea. In fact, before the line swings south the train takes a south-easterly course hugging the banks of the Thames and following the route of the old London & Greenwich Railway. The Greenwich built its railway over a long series of arches as the developers' concern was to bridge the market gardens and pig farms of this 'wretched

district of outer London'. Today the
Brighton train is still carried at rooftop
level through these inner suburbs.

Leaving the station the train skirts
the technically advanced signalbox on
the right. Strikingly austere in looks,
this computerised box controls the
terminus, the threaded maze of
approach, and approximately eight
miles of route on all lines radiating out.
On the Central Division this includes
190 signals and 114 sets of points
stretching west to Clapham on the
South London line and south to Anerley
on the Brighton line. Forty-one trains
can be displayed on the divisional panel
within the signalbox at any one time.

The London Bridge resignalling
scheme cost £21.5 million and took six
years to completion in Spring 1978.
Colour-light signals which were
installed in 1928 were replaced, and
track that since Greenwich days had
been repaired and added to was
completely relaid. While the older
layout had been suitable for steam trains
of different shapes and sizes it proved
quite unacceptable for fast electric
stock. During the period of engineering
the scheme was exasperating for the
traveller, but happily the regular
passenger can hardly have missed the
subsequent lack of operational failures.

Casting a shadow to the northern side
of the signalbox rises the slender 500ft
tower of Guy's Hospital. Guy's was
founded in 1726, on a legacy from
bookseller and speculator Thomas Guy,
who made a fortune in the South Sea
Bubble share boom of 1720. This
showpiece 800-bed teaching hospital is a
city in itself and not only acts as one of
the world's major centres for medical
science, but also as the local hospital for
the surrounding area. The new
development was opened in 1975.

The dull riverside wharves can easily
hide the battleship grey of HMS *Belfast*,
which at 10,553 tons is one of the
biggest ships to have entered the upper
Pool. Launched on 17 March 1938 by
Mrs Neville Chamberlain, her
complement was 850 men. During
World War II the cruiser had a fine
record, including engaging the enemy at
the Battle of the North Cape, (the
sinking of the *Scharnhorst*) and in June
1944, she led the heavy bombardment
supporting the Allied landings on the
beaches of Normandy. Her active
service ended in 1964 and in September
1971 she was moved to the Thames and
opened as a floating museum.

Still looking left, the great mass of
Tower Bridge, its spires tipped bright
gold, identifies the course of London's
river. The bridge, which is symbolic of
Britain throughout the world was
opened in 1894, cost £800,000 and took
nine years to build. It was felt that a new
bridge was necessary to help relieve
congestion in crossing the Thames, but
at the same time it could not become a
barrier to tall ships wanting to enter the
upper Pool. The designers thought up
the novel idea of a double drawbridge.
Two bascules (great leaves) each
weighing over 1000 tons are raised by
machinery housed in the flanking
towers. Raising the heavy bascules takes
$1\frac{1}{2}$ minutes, which surely must be a
lasting tribute to the excellence of
Victorian engineering.

A mile beyond Sarsons Brewery,
where malt vinegar has been produced
for 150 years, and to the east of the
Brighton Railway, a golden dragon
stands sentinel above the church of St
James. The church was built in 1827 to
commemorate the Battle of Waterloo
and the church bells were cast from
captured French guns. Skirting the
lineside is Peak Frean's factory with its
commanding digital clock, which has
become an essential timepiece for both
train crew and traveller alike, while a
branch viaduct snakes south-west
taking the South London line to such
nearby places as East Dulwich and
Peckham Rye.

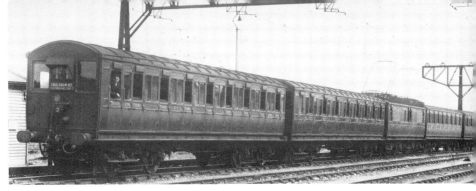

Top: *Overhead electric with 6,700 volts ac as adopted by the LBSCR and extended to Coulsdon by the SR for services from Victoria* (Lens of Sutton)

Centre: *Purley. A London Bridge–Tattenham Corner/Caterham train waits at platform 6 while being divided on 30 May 1951*
(Pamlin Prints)

Bottom: *Suburban electric Maunsell 'bullet nose' set No 4314 is seen at Anerley on 29 May 1950*
(Pamlin Prints)

From this arched spur, the South Bermondsey spur, another viaduct feeds back to the main line thus forming a complete loop. This half-mile loop is frequently used during rush hours to 'stack' fast coast trains awaiting a 'clear' on the main Brighton line. The signal indicator at 'B' on the platform at London Bridge warns the driver that he will be taking this route.

As the South London line peels south-west, the Brighton line eases slightly south and the Kent Coast line breaks away to the east. This is the site of the old Corbett's Lane Junction, an area closely associated with the early days of railway history, signalling and train identification. Track belonging to the various companies met at this blustery spot, and to enable the pointsmen to switch trains to the correct course signs were carried on the front of the locomotives to indicate their routes. Additionally, to help pointsmen distinguish an approaching train, a tall climbing frame was erected by the side of the line and soon this gantry, the forerunner of the signalbox, was nicknamed 'Corbett's Lane Lighthouse'. The practice of locomotive route identification remains today and the destination of most Southern trains is described by the headcode they carry.

Between the Brighton line and the Kent Coast track sprawls the Elizabeth Industrial Estate, while to the west the United Glass Company's miniature bottle factory straddles a bank that once sheltered the Grand Surrey Canal. The canal ran from Surrey Docks at Rotherhithe to form a water link with the south-west suburbs and included a nine mile arm to Croydon, which in 1801 with a population of 5,743 was a rapidly growing market town and centre for the farming lands of East Surrey. The canal flourished during the Georgian period of canal mania and was a source of delight to the neighbouring population offering 'pleasant rows

through beautiful country'.

Eventually, the waterway, which was in direct competition with the Surrey Iron Railway, fell into disuse and much of its bed was used as a foundation for the railway line from New Cross Gate to Norwood. The last traces of the canal were filled and re-opened as a road in January 1980, although the towpath is still maintained and is clearly visible.

New Cross Gate is an important railway centre. At one time a perpetual cloud of thick white steam hung above the busy locomotive shed. Today, the wide sidings, with their modern cleaning machinery, that will either apply a normal wash or clean badly soiled stock with a solution of acid, are used mainly for accommodating empty commuter trains.

A branch of the London Transport East London line terminates at the easterly platform 1 of the five-platform British Rail Station. The short six-station East London line runs from here and its other terminus, New Cross, to Shoreditch, passing under the Thames between Rotherhithe and Wapping. The Thames tunnel completed in 1843 was the first tunnel for public traffic driven under a river. Designed by Sir Marc Brunel, father of Isambard Kingdom Brunel, it was originally intended to connect the LBSCR with the Great Eastern Railway main lines into Liverpool Street. One advantage of the railway has been in the movement of local labour towards the London Docks. These days it forms part of the Metropolitan line, and London Transport has fixed illustrated panels at Wapping Station to chronicle the complex history of both tunnel and line.

Leaving New Cross Gate the 1 in 100 climb up Forest Bank to Forest Hill begins and a clearly defined pattern can be seen in the converging four-line track. From east to west the lines form the down slow, down fast, up fast and up slow. Modern electrics make light work of the 2¾-mile climb, so different from the days of steam; in the closing months when British Rail had locomotives to spare the gruff bark of a light pacific would turn to thunder as the locomotive slogged to gain the summit at Forest Hill. When goods trains from Bricklayers Arms or the docks were still common, they often had a second engine pushing at the back to help get the load to Forest Hill.

The ageing, two-platform stations at Brockley and Honor Oak Park are depressing and uninteresting. Midway between the stations the steel girders that reinforce the grass banks mark the base of a series of landslips that took place in the early 1970s. Only 3¾ miles from London, it is surprising the number of primroses that bloom in this deep cutting near suburban Brockley, during early spring. At refurbished Forest Hill the black-and-white signboard solemnly advises when once a porter would cheerily shout 'Alight here for the Horniman Museum'. The Museum deals with the study of man and his environment, and also houses a large and varied collection of musical instruments. In the early nineteenth century Forest Hill crested the tree clad slopes of Great Northwood – nearby Norwood also derived its name from here.

As the train gathers speed pushing deeper into suburbia it flashes past stations serving Sydenham and Penge West. In spring 1982 the up platform at Sydenham was demolished and re-sited 300ft north. When in the early nineteenth century the route of the railway was discussed and planned, the builders negotiated with a certain William Sanderson whose home was called Anerley (Lonely Place). Sanderson offered part of his estate to the company on condition that a station was erected and that it took the name of his house. This was agreed.

Norwood Junction is a large station which, since the earliest days of railway history has remained a vital railway centre. Originally the station was known as 'Jolly Sailor', taking the name of a lineside inn; likewise Forest Hill was called 'Dartmouth Arms'. Norwood is unusual in that a single track separates platforms 1 and 2 and passengers may board and alight from either side. The Luftwaffe was well aware of the importance of the adjoining goods yards and alerted its aircrews to treat them as a primary target in the blitz on London. The British retaliated by siting anti-aircraft guns on the encroaching hills. Today, diesels from Norwood yard (Classes 08, 09, 33, the occasional Class 47 and electro-diesels of Class 73) work freight and Oxted trains.

Within the next mile the train reaches Windmill Bridge, where the bustling Victoria line sweeps in from the west, and the united route heads south for the sea.

Victoria is a recognised meeting place for both traveller and tourist, and for 100 years passengers would rendezvous 'under the clock' until in 1970 the clock was sold to an American restauranteur. The 'Gateway to Europe' teams with claustrophobic Britons boarding boat and Gatwick trains. Add to this holiday-makers and day-trippers packing summer seaside specials and Victoria becomes a cosmopolitan place of airline plastics holdalls and brightly-coloured holiday impedimenta.

The route from Victoria is historically less interesting than the line from London Bridge. It is also the junior by 20 years. Nevertheless, people journeying from London to Brighton think 'Victoria' and since the turn of the century it has remained the route most widely used.

The terminus boasts a full range of amenities including facilities for boat and airline passengers. Until the mid-1960s Victoria held claim to four crack express trains; nowadays the titled trains with all their glitter have gone.

Platforms 1–8 serve the South Eastern division while the remaining eleven are controlled by the Central Division. The £50 million 'Operation Victoria' scheme included the partial rebuilding of the Edwardian station and the laying of new track over Grosvenor Bridge and on the approach to the terminus, for the original layout had withstood the rigours of nearly 80 years of steam and electric trains.

On weekdays Victoria (Central) handles 842 trains, with 135,000 passengers passing through. Workings to and from Victoria are controlled by the new 'Victoria' signalbox at Clapham Junction which also regulates Brighton line train movements south to Norbury, and in all monitors no less than 267 track miles, replaces 36 signalboxes, and governs 70 other stations, including the lesser London terminals of Holborn Viaduct and Blackfriars.

Directly at platform end the half-mile 1 in 61 pull to Grosvenor Bridge was a constant worry in the days of steam, but seldom was a banker used. Today's 1000hp electric multiple-units accelerate and hardly notice the sharp incline. To the east of the approach lies the South Eastern Division carriage sheds, while to the west a garden-encompassed pumping station plots the course of the old Grosvenor Canal. The canal was built in 1725 and flowed for barely half-a-mile from the River Thames at Chelsea to a basin at Victoria. The waterway was used to ship coal and stone to the Capital and take rubbish away, but was finally absorbed upon the enlargement of the railway station in 1899.

Looking east along the Thames in the shadow of Battersea Power Station lies Nine Elms Reach. The power station is under notice of closure and a team of architects is seeking a use for the huge building, with its four landmark chimney towers. Looking west, the

Chelsea Suspension Bridge opened in 1858 spans Chelsea Reach. The more distant bridge is the Albert, which was built in 1873. This peaceful part of the river was immortalised by the paintings of Whistler.

Behind the South Bank towpath spreads the wide expanse of Battersea Park; the one-time fashionable fields were reclaimed from marshy ground and reinforced with soil excavated during the construction of the London Docks. The extensive coach park bordering the riverside stands on the site of Pimlico Station and part of the original station buildings is still used by a road haulage company.

Few trains are scheduled to stop at Battersea Park, which is a pleasant mid-nineteenth century station, desperately in need of renovation. At Battersea Park the Kent Coast and South Eastern suburban lines strike east, through an industrialised district of South London that was deeply rooted in the growth of the railway system and has been connected with train maintenance ever since.

Nine Elms, once a thriving market gardening region, was partly developed by the London & Southampton Railway which in 1838 built its London terminus there. Subsequently, in 1848 the London & South Western Railway extended the line to Waterloo and Nine Elms became an important goods yard on the north side of the line, with facilities for occasional passengers, who included Queen Victoria, and towards the close of the nineteenth century, the cavalry embarking for the Boer War. The yard is rapidly being covered with industrial and commercial development. The new Covent Garden Market now stands on the site of the

4CIG No 7375 heads a 12-coach formation on the down 17.27 London Bridge–Portsmouth Harbour service on 8 April 1981

erstwhile locomotive works and running shed on the south side of the line. Nearby Stewarts Lane remains an important railway depot, and was responsible for the boat trains, including the Golden Arrow and Night Ferry.

Flying over the South Western main line from Waterloo the Brighton tracks abruptly change course to sweep down to run alongside the West of England lines at Pouparts Junction.

It is at Pouparts Junction but on the north side of the Brighton line tracks that a spur to the West London line heads north east and curves round to the north-west under the South Western main line taking through trains, such as the Brighton–Manchester service, to Kensington, Willesden, Old Oak Common and places beyond. The new Victoria signalling centre has been built between Pouparts and Clapham Junction and stands well back from the railway, partly hidden by the large advertisement hoardings. Clapham Junction is one of the most famous railway junctions in the world. It is certainly the busiest with 2,391 trains passing every 24 hours, and with 17 curving platforms it covers a greater acreage than any other British station. Most Southern Region locomotive-hauled rolling stock is serviced at Clapham Junction and a fair assortment of diesel locomotives can usually be seen there.

Easing south and away from the spawning tentacles of the South Western tracks the Brighton line winds the 1 in 166 gradient through leafy Wandsworth Common. Until Windmill Bridge is reached the railway establishes a set pattern and forms from east to west down slow, up slow, down fast and up fast.

Wandsworth Common, once a busy depot for carriage maintenance, is a pleasant but lightly used station, while Balham generates a far brisker feel, with considerable commuter traffic and interchange facilities, including trains routed south-east along the original Pimlico–Crystal Palace railway line. Balham Station is unusual in that platforms 1 and 2 serving the slow and South London lines were rebuilt in the early 1960s while the little-used platforms 3 and 4 on the main line remain basically in their original style.

Streatham Common, Norbury, Thornton Heath and Selhurst all have extravagant four-platform stations erected around the 1860s but enlarged 40 years later when the line between Clapham Junction and Croydon was quadrupled. Like Balham, the westerly platforms serving the main line are virtually unused, while the other two handle local traffic. At times of operational difficulty the occasional South Coast train calls at Selhurst, as from here lines ply east and west, but generally no long-distance services halt

between Clapham Junction and East Croydon and fast trains pass the former as well. The surburban districts of Streatham and Norbury were developed on middle-class Victorian wealth but twentieth-century inflation has led to the conversion of many of the grandiose houses into flats, and three-bedroomed semi-detached houses have subsequently sprung up on every available spare plot of land. There remains a sprinkling of bright green as several prosperous City banks have meticulously-kept sports grounds around here. Selhurst boasts the largest suburban carriage depot and repair shop on the Central Division.

Ambitious plans for an extensive face-lift for the depot were announced in 1982. The improved workshops will maintain Class 455 suburban units which are due to be introduced to the Central Division in 1986.

South of Selhurst lies a complex of bridges, points, loops and crossovers, known as the Gloucester Road triangle. This hotch potch of tracks was added to piecemeal by the various operating companies and part of the Three Bridges re-signalling scheme includes track modification and a new embankment and flyover between Gloucester Road and Windmill Bridge; 200,000 tonnes of mine waste from Betteshanger Colliery was used to construct the embankment.

East Croydon's six protracted platforms, further lengthened in 1982 and with enhanced signalling all able to handle traffic in either direction, bustle day and night. Croydon was closely connected with the formative days of railway history and nowadays amongst the fine commercial blocks rises the Central Division headquarters. In the 1860s the LBSCR built a spur to serve the town; today all that remains of 'Central Croydon', for this was the name the company gave this shoppers' station, is the brick retaining wall that flanks the northern border of the

A visitor to the Southern Region. A 1750hp English Electric Class 37 locomotive accelerates through Purley Oaks with an Inter-regional train of oil wagons, on 13 June 1981

colourful Town Hall gardens. Five lines link Windmill Bridge with South Croydon, which, as suburban stations go, is among the best. Built in 1865 the building remains basically in its original state. It had been intended to call the station Croham Hurst — taking the name of a popular stretch of neighbouring woodland and in the past the station acted as a terminus for suburban trains.

Shortly beyond the station the Oxted line slips gently east, while Brighton trains ride south on an embankment, which, in 1947 witnessed a major railway disaster. The morning of 24 October was dull and foggy with visibility restricted to around 50 yards. The morning rush was at its peak and London trains were running late. In the general confusion the signalman at Purley Oaks forgot the packed 07.33 from Haywards Heath, halted by his up signal; and remember he couldn't see! When he was offered the 08.04 from Tattenham Corner, crammed with a 1,000 passengers aboard, he found that his Sykes apparatus was locked at danger and he suspected that the instrument had failed. Releasing the mechanism the signal cleared for both the waiting Haywards Heath and the fast approaching local train. Thirty-two people, including the driver of the Tattenham Corner train were killed.

Purley Oaks is a late Victorian station with an extravagant but little used booking hall. The story is told that when the station was being constructed a visiting official questioned a ganger as to the name of a bordering farm. 'Purley Oaks,' he was told. 'Then that is what we will call our station,' the official replied. Another railwayman's tale recalls that the station is haunted, and

that on dark and stormy nights a ghostly top-hatted traveller lurks between platforms 2 and 3.

Purley station was opened in 1841 as Godstone Road. Subsequently, when the branch to Caterham was laid it became Caterham Junction and finally in 1880 it was renamed Purley, to be rebuilt at the end of the century. During these teething years the station was the kernel of much argument and intrigue. Continual squabbling broke out between the station owners, LBSCR, and the company which built the Caterham branch, ending in bankruptcy for that unfortunate concern. Part of the frustration hinged over difficulties in attracting passengers to use the branch, for the Brighton timed its London trains to pull out as the Caterham connection pulled in!

As the Brighton train leaves Purley, the Caterham/Tattenham Corner line slips east. This branch soon divides, the Caterham arm continuing east along the valley, while the Tattenham Corner line passes back under the Brighton tracks, then hurries to Smitham where it curves west to wander lazily through the peaceful Chipstead Valley. In pre-grouping days the Caterham/Tattenham Corner branches formed part of the South Eastern Railway and by a somewhat irrational quirk are today the only regular Central Division trains that terminate at Charing Cross. The trains serving the branches split at Purley and only two minutes are allowed in the timetable for the uncoupling and dispatching the separated portions.

Before the railway reaches Coulsdon the four Brighton lines divide into pairs. The easterly two form the slower line, feeding stations at Coulsdon South, Merstham and Redhill, while the second two quickly bridge this stopping line to become the more easterly pair. Deliberately avoiding all stations including the busy junction at Redhill, this pair creates a fast less hindered route towards the Channel Coast. This $6\frac{1}{2}$-mile loop is aptly named Quarry, for this is a region of deep high-banked cuttings where the railway climbs the 1 in 165 gradient through the North Downs, plunges into the dark hills at Quarry Tunnel (1·2 miles – an adjacent tunnel, similar in length, runs parallel on the stopping line) then makes a short swift dash passing beneath the town of Redhill (Redhill Tunnel 0.4 miles) to rejoin the direct line at Earlswood, two miles south of Redhill.

At Coulsdon South, rising west behind the attractive two-platform station (South Eastern Railway 1899) stands Cane Hill Hospital, while to the left the slopes of Farthing Downs mark the eastern sky. The 500 acres of Farthing Downs and the adjoining common land are owned partly by the London Borough of Croydon and partly by the Corporation of London. The

Downs are riddled with pretty paths and nature trails that tumble in different directions.

Around Merstham the ostentatious concrete motorway scars the lovely Vale of Holmesdale, where the Pilgrims' Way from Winchester to Canterbury ambles timelessly by. Merstham – once called Mesterham – the village where William Cobbett travelling the Brighton Road in 1832 could find little of interest other than 'A field of cabbages', claims notoriety on two counts. Firstly, locally quarried stone was used in the construction of many well-known buildings, including Windsor Castle and the old London Bridge. Secondly, the world's first public railway, the Surrey Iron Railway, (built 1799/1805) with horses providing the motive power, ran from Merstham to Wandsworth via Croydon. One of the prime considerations when planning this railway was the advantage in transporting stone to the Thames for shipment elsewhere. The railway was unusual in that it was the rails that were flanged and not the wagon wheels. This meant the trucks could be pushed directly from rail to road, and vice-versa. Merstham BR station is of pleasing South Eastern design.

Redhill, famous for sand, bricks and Fuller's Earth, was named after the character of its soil. Opened in 1841 as Red Hill and Reigate Road, the station remains an important junction, for it is here that diesel trains on the Reading–Tonbridge service intersect the Brighton line, while diesels on the Gatwick–Reading link join the South Coast tracks. The Gatwick diesel multiple-units previously operated from Paddington and are of standard Western Region types – Gloucester Carriage & Wagon Co/Leyland cross-country units. The units commenced their new rail/air link duties in May 1980 and provided a new sight on the Brighton line. One of the most remarkable workings occurred on 20 May 1980, when during the early evening two of these sets made their way from Redhill to Victoria as an empty train and then formed the 18.38 semi-fast to Brighton. Homegoing commuters must have found their new surroundings very strange!

Setting out from Earlswood, where the station was enlarged as part of the Quarry loop line scheme, two factors become apparent from the train window – the flatness of the land, which obviously led to the siting of Gatwick

A three-car Reading line diesel multiple-unit picks-up at Redhill on 8 May 1981

Airport and which somewhat ironically can result in troublesome fog persisting all day, and the intensive industrial development between the railway and the Brighton Road to the west, whilst the eastern side has resisted man's attack on nature. The regular traveller will also be aware that until the end of quadruple tracks before the mouth of Balcombe Tunnel that fast trains routed via Quarry keep to the through easterly road, while stopping services remain to the west. Generally trains on the faster line build up speeds touching 90mph on the gentle fall from the summit at Quarry Tunnel to the dip near Horley, where the driver will be well prepared to meet the five-mile climb towards the Weald.

Salfords' shanty-like two-platform station holds little interest apart from extensive north-westerly views to the grassy slopes of Box Hill. Even more distant rises Leith Hill, which at 965ft is the highest point of Southern England.

Busy Horley is half-way house on the Brighton Railway and the town boasts an imposing station with four fine platforms and a commodious booking hall. Nine years after the line had opened, the journey to London took 65 minutes and the single third-class fare was the equivalent of 13p. In 1969 the journey took 43 minutes and a single second-class fare cost 35p. In 1983 travelling time for a fast train was reduced to 35 minutes but the second-class fare had rocketed to £2.80. Horley, like so many of the country towns on the Surrey/Sussex border, lies in the noise shadow of Gatwick Airport.

Nowadays the railway at Gatwick grows in harmony with its illustrious neighbour and many cash-starved

station managers must feel that money is all too readily channelled here. In fact it appears that Gatwick is a magic word in railway circles, for in 1979 £10.7 million was budgeted for the redevelopment of the station, which included a moving walkway to London's second international airport. The station originally known as Gatwick racecourse closed in 1935, to re-open in 1958 as Gatwick Airport. The vital challenge of the airport and its needs has introduced a spread of stock and locomotives from the other Regions, including the Western Region diesel multiple-units and the more exciting locomotive-hauled Manchester trains. The locomotives rostered to work this service provide a variety which for many years had been absent from the Brighton line, and amongst others 47 500 *Great Western* and 47 580 *County of Essex*, have hauled these trains. As the railway passes the turgid cargo hangers, look right across the main runway to the spire of pretty St Michael & All Angels church at Lowfield Heath and contemplate the choir singing with full voice as a climbing jet screams by! The architect responsible for the church was distressed when his dog was killed chasing a ball, by a passing horse and cart. Carved in stone on the south wall a dog, clutching a ball, looks down.

Three Bridges is a bustling junction with extensive freight yards, and it is here the mid-Sussex line strikes west. Until the early 1960s a branch ran east from here to East Grinstead and Tunbridge Wells. Three Bridges can be likened to several other Brighton stations in that the LBSCR curiously avoided established towns and generated such settlements as Haywards Heath, which in time has grown into an important place with a population today of 16,000.

A £14 million contract was signed on 25 March 1980 between British Rail and the Westinghouse Brake & Signal Co Ltd, which included the supply and installation of equipment for the ultra-modern signalling centre to be erected at Three Bridges. The new installation is to replace 33 old signalboxes and control a total of 280 track miles, stretching north to Anerley and Thornton Heath, and south to the coast. Three Bridges Box also monitors all workings on the Tattenham Corner and the Caterham branches, the Oxted line to Woldingham, the Tonbridge line around Redhill, the Mid-Sussex line as far as Faygate, the Eastbourne line to Plumpton and the Coastways link between Falmer and Hove.

The Brighton line resignalling scheme when completed in 1987 will have cost British Rail £45.7 million and with complementary systems operative at London Bridge and Victoria, a total expenditure of around £150 million is envisaged. By 1987 the entire length of railway between Capital and coast will be controlled by the three centres and the line will possess one of the most advanced colour-light signalling installations in the world. British Rail's automatic warning system, which both visually and audibly alerts the driver, and acts as a safety back-up to external signalling, is included in the overall plan. Considerable remodelling of track layout is also programmed and modification to certain platforms at Norwood Junction, East Croydon, Purley, Redhill, Earlswood, Three Bridges and Brighton is being undertaken, in some instances including lengthening platforms to facilitate use by 12-coach trains. Upon completion it is estimated that the journey time for a fast down passenger train will be cut by six minutes, whereas the up service will benefit by an improvement of five minutes.

Climbing through the Sussex Weald the line cuts Tilgate Forest, which, together with the neighbouring 200-acre recreational park, forms part of the Ashdown Ridge. Among the many natural amenities the Forest Park also contains a well-organised field centre, a boating lake and a miniature zoo. Tilgate lake is thought to have been developed for the iron industry and more recently was owned by Sir Malcolm Campbell, who used it for flotation trials.

Although still heavily wooded, the Wealden Forest has been vastly reduced since the time of the Saxon invasion when the word 'Wald' meaning forest, was used. During the Middle Ages rich deposits of iron-ore were found in the Weald and a major iron industry developed in the hills. The industry declined owing to a combination of circumstances, including a severe drought during the first half of the eighteenth century, scarcity of fuel following indiscriminate deforestation, the near exhaustion of ore, and lastly the production of coal in the north, which provided an alternative form of energy to charcoal.

Scenically, the stretch of railway from Tilgate through the Weald to Haywards Heath is the most attractive on the line; certainly the view from the Ouse Valley Viaduct excels. North of Balcombe Tunnel (0.7 miles) quadruple tracks end. At one stage the LBSCR had plans to extend the four lines through to the coast, but the estimated cost of rebuilding the Ouse Viaduct and the widening of four tunnels proved too great an expense for the company to bear. The convergence of the fast and slow lines to one up and one down can cause irritating delays, although alterations to track layout in 1981 permitted faster running towards the tunnel mouth.

Balcombe, a pretty little country village is served by an equally pretty two-platform station. Of classical Moccatta 'Brighton' design the station, other than for the erection of an ugly

The northern portal of Clayton Tunnel in the spring of 1981. Incorporated in the top of the structure is a house!

concrete bridge, has changed little since it was built in 1841.

John Rastrick's Ouse Viaduct is among the most impressive feats of railway engineering in Britain. Strangely, the passenger is hardly aware that he is bridging the fertile valley as the train speeds south, and to appreciate the full grace of the 37 arch viaduct it is best to view it from afar. Nearly 100ft below, a shallow River Ouse winds through Sussex meadows to meet the sea at Newhaven, 25 river miles south-east. It is astonishing to contemplate that much of the material used in the construction of the great viaduct was brought directly to the site by boat.

The surrounding countryside epitomises Sussex, and of especial beauty are the gardens at Wakehurst Place, operated jointly by the National Trust and Kew Gardens, and the picture-postcard village of Lindfield.

Busy Haywards Heath station, with its four platforms, stands on an embankment overlooking the town, and is of pure 'Southern Electric' design. Passengers for the Bluebell Railway for a year or two would alight at Haywards Heath and take the branch electric train to Horsted Keynes, the Bluebell's northern terminus. The branch, diverged at Copyhold Junction, 1¼ miles north of Haywards Heath, and went via Ardingly; it closed in 1963. Nowadays, passengers are conveyed to the Bluebell Railway by Southdown bus to Sheffield Park (the south end of the line).

Leaving Haywards Heath the railway slips through Folly Tunnel (0.1 miles) and upon re-entering daylight a noticeable transition takes place in the passing scene as the thickly-timbered hills of the Weald give way to a lush lowland plain.

Wivelsfield's pleasantly rural station was opened as Keymer Junction, for it is at Keymer, slightly south of Wivelsfield, that the main Eastbourne line branches east.

Nearby Burgess Hill is served by an equally attractive mid-Victorian station, while Hassocks, on the climb to Clayton Tunnel, has a much newer cast-concrete building. Both these stations were built primarily to feed the surrounding downland villages that during the years and because of the railway have become somewhat suburban. It is interesting to note that to satisfy this demand for commuter traffic several fast rush-hour trains now call at these stations and that during the day hourly Victoria stopping services and regular semi-fast buffet-car trains call. In March 1980, British Rail's first lady station manager took charge of these two stations.

At Clayton the railway bursts the great chalk fortress of the South Downs. Before the train plunges into the gloom of the line's longest tunnel (1.3 miles) it is possible to glimpse the windmill landmarks of Jack and Jill high above on Clayton Hill. Jack is the black tower mill, without sails, and Jill the white post mill. The South Downs rise and fall from Beachy Head to the chalklands of Hampshire, and along much of their spine and crossing Clayton Hill runs the glorious South Downs Way. East of Clayton stands Ditchling Beacon; to the west broods Devil's Dyke.

Careful consideration was given to the possibility of a 'South Downs National Park', but after much discussion and thought it was felt that the amenities offered did not match the requirements sought. However, the whole Sussex escarpment, threaded by the river valleys of Adur, Arun, Cuckmere and Ouse is designated as an Area of Outstanding Natural Beauty.

Clayton Tunnel is one of the most remarkable engineering jobs on the Brighton Railway. The northern limit of the tunnel is embellished with a grand gothic façade that would enhance a medieval palace. Why such unnecessary expense was incurred is difficult to understand especially as the traveller sees little of this edifice from the train window. Directly above the tunnel mouth sits an occupied cottage, which surely ought to be the home of a train spotter!

On the bright Sunday morning of 25 August 1861 Clayton was the scene of a shocking accident, certainly amongst the worst in the history of the Brighton line. Coming from Brighton, Clayton Tunnel is approached by a long winding incline, Patcham Tunnel, and a series of dark cuttings, as the railway labours on a five-mile journey from the sea. Three London trains had left Brighton station within seven minutes of each other; all three were running late and all three were of particularly heavy formation, with 16, 17 and 12 coaches respectively. The unpredictable action of the staff at Brighton station in dispatching three trains at such short interval, especially when allowance is made for the unsophisticated signalling equipment in use at the time with little communication, must be questioned. After the first train passed the up distant signal protecting Clayton Tunnel, the

primitive mechanism failed to return to danger, and when to his horror the signalman at Clayton South saw the second approaching train he seized a red flag but doubted if the driver had seen the hurried warning. The driver had, and braked with full might, albeit the tremendous weight carried his train a further half-mile. The driver guessed there must be trouble ahead and decided to reverse to the tunnel mouth. Meanwhile the signalbox at Clayton North confirmed on the telegraph to Clayton South that the train had passed, but this of course related to the first of the three trains, and when to his surprise the signalman at Clayton South saw the third London train he cheerfully waved it on; the driver acknowledged and picked up speed. Twenty-one people died in the terror of a tunnel disaster as the third train hit the second.

Two miles further south was the downland setting of another serious accident but on this occasion of far more recent date. On the evening of 19 December 1978 all trains were heavily delayed. It had been an exasperating day for the Division, culminating in a track circuit failure, a faulty conductor rail and a spiteful bomb hoax at Victoria, all of which resulted in certain re-scheduling, including the 12-coach 21.50 Victoria–Brighton service running ahead of the eight-coach 21.40 Victoria–Littlehampton train. To make matters worse a 73-year-old lady passenger who had been enjoying a little seasonal festivity wandered onto the line at Brighton Station and the current had to be switched-off while she was escorted back to safety. This mishap resulted in the Brighton train being halted at the down signal protecting Patcham Tunnel. The following Littlehampton train, now running nearly an hour late, passed a single yellow 'caution' signal, but for some unknown reason did not appreciably reduce speed. The next signal, protecting the Brighton train,

was the crucial one for it should have displayed a red aspect. But it was in darkness, for a bulb had failed and the Littlehampton train continued at high speed, its driver having missed the absent signal. Even after an emergency brake application, the Littlehampton unit was travelling at an estimated 45mph when it struck the tail of the leading train. Three people, including the driver of the 21.40 were killed. The damage to both sets was extensive and the line remained closed for several days. It was this accident which emphasised the dated pre-war signalling equipment in use on the line and hastened implementation of the massive re-signalling programme. Normally in modern signalling a lamp failure is detected and automatically puts the previous signal to danger. But the 45 year old signalling system still in use then did not have this added safety feature.

Patcham Tunnel (0.3 miles) is the final barrier as the train races on, beckoned by the sparkle of the sea. Preston Park is a rather brash, refurbished four-platform station, serving a pleasant but generously-populated part of northern Brighton. Leaving Preston Park the Worthing line branches west on the Cliftonville Curve, while the Brighton train passes the former Pullman workshops. These were originally sited at Battersea, moved to Preston Park in 1928 and were operative for 38 years. In their heyday

An eight-coach 4CIG/4BIG leaves Brighton Station as the 11.34 East Croydon and Victoria service, on 29 May 1981, while a Class 73 electro-diesel, a 12-coach train of 4CIGs and a 4VEP unit stand in the sidings

the depot could accommodate 19 coaches at any one time.

On the down side at Montpelier Junction, John Rastrick's magnificent 27-arch London Road Viaduct sweeps east taking the 'Coastways' rail service to the seaside towns of Seaford, Eastbourne, Hastings and Ore. The viaduct, which was completed in 1846 and took only ten months to build, received a direct hit by German bombs during World War II.

Brighton Station's 900-vehicle car park is the largest operated by the Southern Region and stands on the levelled site of the renowned locomotive works. Rationalisation during the 1930s brought a gradual decline to the depot, as it was Southern Railway policy to switch all major development to Ashford and Eastleigh, but in 1940 the works was re-tooled and subsequently thrived until 1957. The last steam locomotive to be constructed at Brighton was BR Class 4 2–6–4T No 80154.

Discounting the prestigious London termini, the fine 1840 station at Brighton merits place amongst the best in the land. The building was designed

ROUTE MILEAGES AND TYPICAL JOURNEY TIMES: VICTORIA–EAST CROYDON–BRIGHTON

Date: 6 April 1981
Headcode: 4
12 coaches: Class 421/1 (4 CIG) 7318, 7320
Class 420/1 (4 BIG) 7044
Driver: W. Knight

Station	*Opened*	*Platforms*	*Miles From VIC/ To BTON*	*Lines joining route*	*Schedule times*	*Actual times*	*Speed (mph)*	*Checks*
Victoria	1860	19	0/51	Interchange for Kent Coast and continent	10-08	10-09½		Signals
Battersea Park	1867	5	1¾/49¼			10-12½	35	
Clapham Junction	1863	17	2¾/48¼	Interchange for Waterloo–Portsmouth/ Bournemouth/Salisbury/ Exeter		10-14	40	
Wandsworth Common	1869	4	4/47			10-15	45	
Balham	1856	4	4¾/46¼	South London line– Sutton/Horsham		10-16	45	Restriction
Streatham Common	1862	4	6¼/44¾			10-19½	20	Restriction
Norbury	1878	4	7½/43½			10-20½	55	
Thornton Heath	1862	4	8¾/42¼			10-22	62	
Selhurst	1865	4	9½/41½	West Croydon/ Norwood Junction		10-23	10	Signals
East Croydon	1841	6	10½/40½	London Bridge/ Victoria interchange	Arr. 10-22 Dep 10-23	10-25½ 10-26½		
South Croydon	1865	5	11½/39½	Junction for Oxted line		10-28	50	
Purley Oaks	1899	4	12½/38½			10-28¾	70	
Purley	1841	6	13½/37½	Tattenham Corner/ Caterham		10-30	62	
Coulsdon North (Quarry)		—	—			10-33	30	Restriction
Coulsdon South	1899	2	15¼/35¾			—	—	Via Quarry
Merstham	1844	2	19/32			—	—	Via Quarry
Redhill	1841	3 (plus goods)	21/30	Reading/Tonbridge		—	—	Via Quarry
Earlswood	1868	4	21¾/29¼			10-40	52	
Salfords	1915	2	23¾/27¼			10-42	64	
Horley	1841	4	26/25			10/43½	80	
Gatwick Airport	1958	6	26¾/24¼			10-44	81	
Three Bridges	1844	5	29½/21½	Mid-Sussex		10-46	75	
Balcombe	1841	2	34/17			10-50¼	84	
Haywards Heath	1841	4	38/13			10-54	30	Restriction
Wivelsfield	1886	2	40¾/10¼			10-57	74	
(*Keymer Junction*)	—	—	41¼/9¾	Lewes/Newhaven/ Eastbourne/Hastings				
Burgess Hill	1841	2	41¾/9¼			10-58½	76	
Hassocks	1841	2	43¾/7¼			10-59¾	70	
Preston Park	1869	4	49½/1½	Worthing/Littlehampton		11-04	10	Signals
Brighton	1840	9	51/0	Coastways	11-06	11-07		

ROUTE MILEAGES: LONDON BRIDGE TO NORWOOD JUNCTION

Station	*Opened*	*Platforms*	*Miles from LB to BTON*	*Lines joining route*
London Bridge	1836	16	0/51	Interchange Charing Cross/ Cannon Street/Kent Coast
New Cross Gate	1839	5	2¾/48¼	LT Metropolitan (East London line)
Brockley	1871	2	3¾/47¼	
Honor Oak Park	1886	2	4¾/46¼	
Forest Hill	1839	2	5½/45½	
Sydenham	1839	2	6½/44½	Crystal Palace
Penge West	1839	2	7/44	
Anerley	1839	2	7½/43½	
Norwood Junction	1839	7	8½/42½	Victoria/West Croydon/ Sutton

by David Moccatta and although certain modifications and improvements have been made to the spacious terminus with its nine curving platform, it retains most of the original structure – the grand roof gives particular pleasure. It is easy to see how the building impressed the Victorians and fitted so snugly within the bountiful image that the town had managed to create. The handsome train indicator board on the central concourse was moved from Victoria in 1927, having served at that London station since 1908. Three trains an hour leave Brighton on the 'Coastways' line routed west towards Bognor and Portsmouth, while a similar number radiate east. Four trains an hour feed the main London line; among the more unusual departures in the 1983 summer service on the line to the west are the Friday and Saturday trains to Penzance, although only one returns to Brighton, the other going to Waterloo. The Saturday train runs in winter to Plymouth. In more halcyon times this train worked daily via Okehampton and

was one of two westerly cross-country trains, the other running to Bournemouth. A similar Saturday service operates today to Cardiff.

Sadly, the seaside resort of Brighton has lost the euphoria once generated by the carefree family on their well-earned summer rest and much of the panache has gone. However, the splendid Marina, the contemporary Conference Centre and the growing army of visitors arriving from Continental Europe are bringing a fresh vitality to the town. Perhaps the Southern Region could help Brighton in the struggle to regain the coveted accolade as premier holiday resort of the 'Sunny South' by re-introducing a named express, upgrading catering facilities on fast trains and establishing a wider network of routes to the furthermost parts of the British Isles. Might we even see a revamped Brighton Belle Pullman? If it can be done as a charter train between London and Folkestone as part of the re-created Venice–Simplon–Orient Express why not between London and Brighton?

Bibliography

Most of the material in this book comes from a lifetime's interest and study of British Railways. Libraries are well stocked with references and railway literature. Of particular interest for further reading to those wanting to find out more on the Brighton line, its history, motive power, train services, indeed all its aspects, I would recommend:

The Railways of Southern England – Main Lines, Edwin Course, (Batsford)

A Regional History of the Railways of Great Britain, Vol 2 Southern England, Vol 3 Greater London, H. P. White (David & Charles)

Steam Locomotives of British Rail, H. C. Casserley (Hamlyn)

Sir Herbert Walker's Southern Railway, C. F. Klapper (Ian Allan)

The Story of British Railways, Barrington Tatford (Sampson Low)

The London to Brighton Line 1841–1977, Adrian Gray (The Oakwood Press)

Famous Trains (The Southern Belle), Cecil J. Allen

The London Brighton & South Coast Railway, C. Hamilton Ellis (Ian Allan)

Southern Electric, G. T. Moody (Ian Allen)

150 Years of Railway Carriages, Geoffrey Kichenside (David & Charles)

Pullman, Julian Morel (David & Charles)

British Railway Signalling, G. M. Kichenside & A. R. Williams (Ian Allan)
Red for Danger, L. T. C. Rolt (with additional material by Geoffrey Kichenside) (David & Charles)

For current developments the monthly magazines *Modern Railways*, *Railway World*, *Railway Magazine*, and *Railway Gazette* are invaluable.

Acknowledgements

Many people have helped with material, advice and comments but in particular I would thank the British Rail staff, especially those in the Public Relations Office at Waterloo.

Croydon, March 1983

John Eddolls

British Library Cataloguing in Publication Data

Eddolls, G. J.
   The Brighton line.
   1. British Rail – Southern Region
   2. Railways – England – History
   I. Title
   385'.09422   HE3020.B/
   ISBN 0–7153–8251–9

Photoset in Plantin by
Northern Phototypesetting Co Bolton Lancs.
Printed in Great Britain by
A. Wheaton & Co. Ltd., Exeter
for David & Charles (Publishers) Ltd.
Brunel House Newton Abbot Devon

Published in the United States of America
by David & Charles Inc.
North Pomfret Vermont 05053 USA